SPOTLIGHT
ON CHILDREN'S
AUTHORS

KATE DICAMILLO

SUE CORBETT

Cavendish
Square

New York

Published in 2014 by Cavendish Square Publishing, LLC
303 Park Avenue South, Suite 1247, New York, NY 10010

Library of Congress Cataloging-in-Publication Data

Corbett, Sue.
Kate DiCamillo / Sue Corbett.
pages cm.—(Spotlight on children's authors)
Summary: "Presents the biography of children's book author Kate DiCamillo while exploring her creative process as a writer and the cultural impact of her work"—Provided by publisher.
Includes bibliographical references and index.
ISBN 978-1-60870-933-5 (hardcover)—ISBN 978-1-62712-141-5 (paperback)—ISBN 978-1-60870-940-3 (ebook)
1. DiCamillo, Kate—Juvenile literature. 2. Authors, American—21st century—Biography—Juvenile literature.
3. Children's stories—Authorship—Juvenile literature. I. Title.
PS3604.I23Z63 2013
813'.6—dc23

Senior Editor: Deborah Grahame-Smith
Art Director: Anahid Hamparian
Series Designer: Kay Petronio

Photo research by Linda Aveilhe
Cover photo courtesy of Tom Sweeney/ZUMA Press/Corbis

The photographs in this book with permission and through courtesy of:
Allen Brisson-Smith/The New York Times/Redux: p. 4; Courtesy of Kate DiCamillo: p. 6; Ron Buskirk/Alamy : p. 10; Joe Rossi/KRT/Newscom: p. 12; Copyright © 1995 Christopher Paul Curtis. Delacorte Press, a division of Random House Children's Books Inc.: p. 14; Copyright © 2000 by Kate DiCamillo. Candlewick Press, Somerville, MA.: p. 16, 20; Gary Lee/UPPA/ZUMA Press/Newscom: p. 24; Handout/KRT/Newscom: p. 27; Jim Smeal/BEImages/Rex USA: p. 30; Everett Collection: p. 32; Tom Sweeney/ZUMA Press/Corbis: p. 34; Copyright © 2012 by Kate DiCamillo, illustrated by Yoko Tanaka. Candlewick Press, Somerville, MA.: p. 36; Copyright © 2010 by Kate DiCamillo and Alison McGhee. Illustrations copyright © 2010 by Tony Fucile. Candlewick Press, Somerville, MA.: p. 37

Printed in the United States of America

CONTENTS

INTRODUCTION: How to Warm Up During a Minnesota Winter

The winter of 1996 to 1997 was one of the coldest ever in Minneapolis. After ice storms in November, a rolling barrage of blizzards dropped nearly 40 inches of snow from mid-December through January.

Kate DiCamillo, who had moved to Minnesota two years earlier, simply could not get warm. She was missing Florida. She had grown up in Clermont, a small town west of Orlando.

"I was homesick," Kate recalled. "You couldn't walk outside without slipping on the ice and cracking your head. And I was missing the sound of Southern people talking." Perhaps worst of all, Kate's apartment building did not allow pets. "So I was also missing having a dog," she added.

Other people might have turned up the thermostat and phoned home. Kate started writing. "I created the biggest, smelliest, friendliest dog I could imagine," she remembered. Then she set him loose in a grocery store in the small (fictional) town of Naomi, Florida, where he first ran into the produce and then ran into a young girl named India Opal Buloni. Like Kate was in Minnesota, the character of Opal is homesick. She has just moved to Naomi with her father, the new minister at the Open Arms Baptist Church. The preacher, as Opal calls her dad, sends her to the store to get food for dinner. She comes back with Winn-Dixie, the dog, named for the supermarket where they found each other. The preacher doesn't want a dog, but Winn-Dixie has a lot of personality—and a smile so wide it makes Opal's dad sneeze— and Opal deserves some happiness. Her mother left the family when her daughter was three, and Opal is still aching over this loss.

As dogs will do, Winn-Dixie nudges Opal out of her shell by getting her out of the house (or trailer, in this case) and into a life of adventure, including, now and again, some innocent trouble.

Kate finished the first draft of Opal's story in twenty-eight days. She titled it *Because of Winn-Dixie*.

What's up, Doc? Kate, age 3, dresses as Bugs Bunny for Halloween in her hometown near Philadelphia, PA.

Chapter 1
A SICKLY KID

Strictly speaking, **Katrina Elizabeth DiCamillo** is not from Florida or Minnesota. She was born in a Pennyslvania hospital near Philadelphia on March 25, 1964.

As a child, Kate was frequently sick. At that time, doctors believed that weather could improve a person's health, so Kate's doctor suggested the family move to a warmer climate. Kate's father, Lou, was an orthodontist in Merion, a Philadelphia suburb. Her mother, Betty, was a schoolteacher. The plan was for Betty to take Kate and Curt, Kate's older brother, to Florida, where the hot sun might ease Kate's chronic pneumonia. Kate's father would follow when he could.

Only he never did.

Lou's absence left a deep impression on Kate. "It's such a defining thing," she said. "It's a hole that you keep trying to fill for the rest of your life."

Kate was five years old when she, Curt, and Betty resettled in Clermont, a small town set on a ridge of gently rolling hills 22 miles west of Orlando. Betty found a teaching job.

Today Central Florida is a popular tourist destination. It is home to Walt Disney World, which opened in 1971, and thousands of hotels, restaurants, and other attractions that sprang up around Disney World to accommodate the millions of people who would vacation there in the coming decades.

But when the DiCamillos arrived in 1969, Central Florida was still a sleepy place where few people lived year-round. Founded in 1884 and named for a town in France, Clermont was known locally as "gem of the hills"—a nickname that not many places in Florida could claim, since most of the state is pancake flat.

Thanks in large part to the growth of tourism, Clermont's population increased exponentially in the 1980s and 1990s, but in 1969 the town still had far more orange trees than residents. Like most of the rest of Lake County, Clermont's major industry was growing citrus fruit. In fact, the first human-constructed landmark in the Orlando area was the 226-foot-tall Citrus Tower, erected on one of the highest hills in Clermont in 1956.

Kate's health did not improve instantly despite the warmer climate. ("Every school picture has [an oozing] red eye," she claimed.) Kate remembers spending many days at home by herself. "My mother would say, 'I'll call you at lunch,' and then forget all about me. I learned to entertain myself."

A lot of that entertainment came from reading. Kate remembers that at the Cooper Memorial Library in downtown Clermont, children were not allowed to borrow more than four books at a time. The library staff waived that limit for Kate. "The librarian, Miss Alice, explained that she knew I was a true reader, so she gave me carte blanche to take out as many books as I wanted," Kate said.

Looking back, Kate now sees how her sickly childhood laid the foundation for her life as a writer. Because she was ill so often, she read "without discretion," she said. "Cereal boxes, instructions on how to work the radio, and absolutely everything in the library." Because she was alone so much, she used stories to nourish her imagination.

The Power of Story

Though Kate was a good student and a well-behaved kid, she did get into Big Trouble once. For her ninth birthday, she received a subscription to *Humpty Dumpty Magazine*, which she loved. In one issue, she read a story that she liked so much, she copied it longhand. She discovered she liked it even more when it was written in her own handwriting. She showed it to her mother, Betty.

"You wrote this?" Betty asked.

"I did," Kate told her. "Because I did write it, didn't I? I mean in the most literal sense, I wrote the story down."

Betty showed it to a neighbor, Kate's teacher, and the school principal, all of whom praised the wonderful story Kate had written.

Kate's teacher, Miss Beltzer, even said, "I think we have a little writer on our hands."

Kate knew she should tell the truth, but "the necessary words—'I did not write it. I copied it. I lied'—would not issue forth from my mouth." And anyway, she didn't really want to tell the truth. "I wanted to be the person who wrote the story," Kate said. "I wanted to be the writer."

She hid the magazine under her mattress.

Then Betty read the story out loud over the phone to Kate's father, Lou. He came to visit immediately. Kate's story was the first thing he mentioned. Kate began to cry.

"Why are you crying?" Lou asked.

Kate remembered thinking, "I am crying because my father, whom I love, dream about, long for, is suddenly, unexpectedly in front of me; and he is there because of the story I did not write. I am crying because I am a liar. I am crying because I am afraid that I will get caught."

And she did get caught. Miss Beltzer read the story again, this time in the pages of *Humpty Dumpty Magazine*.

Kate confessed and begged for forgiveness. She said she had learned her lesson.

"Although it was not, perhaps, the lesson that the adults would have liked me to have I learned. What I learned was this: story is power."

And because she grew up in Florida, she was exposed to a way of talking and storytelling—that she might never have heard if she had grown up in Philadelphia. "I absorbed that Southern cadence which I wouldn't have had access to otherwise," said Kate. "It's a great voice for storytelling."

Despite her illnesses, Kate excelled academically. "I loved school. I loved coloring inside the lines," she remembered. "I went all of kindergarten through twelfth grade just being a really good student. Everything was easy." When she graduated from Clermont High School in 1982, Kate was the salutatorian.

At the University of Florida, Kate majored in English. One of her professors told her she had "a way with words." Another singled out Kate's eye for detail in an essay she wrote about a homeless woman who had asked her for change.

Kate the True Reader made up her mind. She would become a writer.

The Walt Disney Company opened the Epcot Center in 1982, the year Kate graduated from high school.

Only she wasn't sure how to do that.

So instead she looked for a job that would pay the bills but leave her enough mental energy to write in her free time. After her college graduation, she got a job as an usher at Disney World's Epcot Center. "I wore a powder-blue space suit and told people, 'Watch your step,'" Kate said. "That was it, all day long. 'Watch your step, please. Watch your step.'"

Kate also worked as a bingo caller, sold tickets at a place called Circus World, and planted philodendrons at a greenhouse. She recalled, "The whole time I talked incessantly about being a writer and read books about writing and imagined, in great detail, my life as a writer. I did everything except write."

The Kate who had so easily succeeded in school floundered in her twenties. Her friends had gotten jobs and had made progress in their careers, while Kate had written occasionally in her spare time but had lacked the confidence to submit her stories to magazines and publishers.

"It was very hard for my mother to go to the grocery store. I had gone off [from high school] in clouds of glory and now people would ask, 'What's Kate doing?' and my mom would be, 'Oh, um. Y'know. She's working at a campground.'"

By age twenty-nine, Kate was disgusted with herself. "It occurred to me that I could easily spend the rest of my life doing nothing but dreaming," she said. "So I sat down and thought very seriously about exactly what it took to be a writer. I came to the conclusion that one thing, absolutely, was required: writing. And so, scared, uncertain, terrified of failure, I began. I made myself write two pages a day. And in this way, I wrote a short story. It was a very bad short story. I rewrote it. It got marginally better. I rewrote it again. And again. And again. I sent it off to a magazine. They rejected it. And I was in business. Sort of."

Kate does not like to dress up. She's most comfortable in jeans and a T-shirt.

Chapter 2
THE LATE BLOOMER

Shortly after Kate promised herself she would write something every day, a friend who was moving to Minneapolis told Kate that she needed a roommate and asked if Kate wanted to join her.

Kate had spent nearly twenty-five years in a place where the annual snowfall was always exactly the same: zero inches. The average daily temperature in Central Florida is 72 degrees Fahrenheit, and 250 days a year are sunny. Kate did not own a winter coat; she barely even owned any socks.

But she said yes.

"I have never regretted it once, not even when it's 20 below," Kate said. The move jolted her out of the rut she felt she was in. She signed up for writing classes and eventually joined a critique group run by a writer named Jane Resh Thomas. Keeping the commitment she had made to herself, Kate rose faithfully every day at 4 a.m. to write two pages of a story before she had to clock in at her job.

Kate also got a job related to the publishing industry. She worked as a picker at a book wholesaler called the Bookman. A picker fills orders for libraries and bookstores from a warehouse of brand-new books. As fate would have it, Kate was assigned to the third floor, where all the children's books were shelved.

Naturally, the True Reader could not help herself from sampling the wares at work. "I would pick fast and then lock myself in the bathroom and read," she told the audience at the 2010 Miami Book Fair International. With the same discretion she showed as a child reading cereal boxes, she pored through the merchandise—picture books, poetry books, and board books. One day she started reading *The Watsons Go to Birmingham—1963* by Christopher Paul Curtis, a book that, Kate said, "changed my life." She was so intrigued by the first chapter that she checked the book out so she could read the rest at home.

The Watsons Go to Birmingham—1963 was published in 1995. It received a Newbery Honor from the American Library Association—an

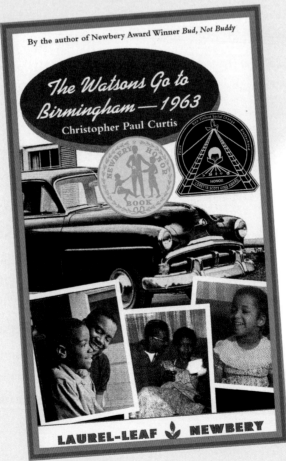

Christopher Paul Curtis's Newbery Honor winner was the book that made Kate want to write for kids.

incredible achievement for Curtis, since *The Watsons* was his first novel and his "real" job was assembling cars at an automotive manufacturing plant. Curtis's book tells the story of an African-American family that lives in Michigan but takes a road trip to Alabama to visit relatives at the height of the civil rights movement. The novel is both very funny and powerfully sad.

"I read it and decided I wanted to try to write a novel for kids," Kate said. She typed out the first ten pages of *The Watsons* to see what it looked like in manuscript form. Kate added, "It's a wonderful exercise for anyone because you learn a lot from doing it."

Then the cold hit. The Minnesota winter of 1996 to 1997 started early, with a mid-November storm that covered the Twin Cities with a half-inch layer of ice. The ice storm was an omen. In December and January, one massive snowfall after another downed trees and power lines, closed schools, and frequently made travel impossible.

Kate longed for sun, bare feet, and other things she loved about Florida—like having enough room to own a dog. Over the course of four weeks, she banged out what she would later call a "hymn of praise to dogs, friendship, and the South." It was a gentle, funny jewel of a story about a girl trying to fill a big hole in her heart—the absence of her mother—and the mangy, lovable mutt who helps her do it. Into India Opal Buloni's sad life, Kate sent quirky, affable souls: a pet-store owner who serenades his animals and a librarian whose father amasses a fortune by manufacturing a candy that tastes both sweet and sorrowful. Opal finds friends in a five-year-old girl and an elderly recluse, both of whom are charmed by Opal's shaggy brown dog.

Kate herself made a friend of Linda Nelson, a saleswoman she met in the elevator at the Bookman. Kate told Linda about her writing,

Kate's first draft of *Because of Winn-Dixie* languished in her publisher's office for months when the editor assigned to read it went on maternity leave and then decided not to return to work.

and Linda offered to pass a picture-book manuscript Kate had written to an editor at her company, Candlewick Press, which is located in Somerville, Massachusetts.

The editor never bought the picture book, but she encouraged Kate to keep submitting her work. Kate sent her the manuscript of her first novel, which then had the title *Because of Winn-Dixie*, but the editor handled only picture books. She promised to pass on the manuscript to a colleague who acquired novels.

In *that* editor's office, Kate's manuscript sat in a pile and gathered dust for a long time. If only Winn-Dixie could have barked! The editor had gone on maternity leave without ever having read the story. Months later, when the editor notified her boss that she had decided not to return to her job at all, a twenty-seven-year-old editorial assistant named Kara LaReau was asked to clean out the editor's office.

"It was just a sea of manuscripts in there," Kara recalled. "I took home boxes of manuscripts every night, declining some outright and apologizing for the delay. I wrote reader reports for the ones that had promise. There weren't many."

Mix-up or Magic?

While Kate was working at the Bookman, she began to learn a little bit about the publishing industry. She knew that for the kind of book she was writing—a middle-grade novel—sales would never be very high. After all, the Bookman typically stocked no more than twelve hardcover copies of most middle-grade novels to serve its distribution area—the entire Midwest! But she vividly remembers one day in 1998, when they unpacked an order and found that a publisher had sent them 1,200 copies of one particular middle-grade novel, instead of the usual 12. "I remember thinking, 'Oh man, someone messed up,'" Kate said.

Nobody had heard of the book they unpacked—yet. It was *Harry Potter and the Sorcerer's Stone.*

Then she found *Because of Winn-Dixie*. "I realized very quickly that whoever had written it knew how to tell a story," Kara said. "I ended up writing a highly enthusiastic reader report, desperately passionate, with an abundance of capital letters and exclamation points. The whole tone was something like, 'Please, please, please. Can we sign this book up immediately?'"

Because Kara was an editorial assistant at the time (she now owns her own creative consulting company, Bluebird Works), she did not have the authority to buy Kate's story herself. Her boss, Liz Bicknell, liked the manuscript, too, but wanted to know if Kate was willing to revise it.

Kate was.

A willingness to revise is essential to being a successful writer, especially for novelists. It is hard to see the forest for the trees when you have written a novel; the story may make perfect sense to the person who has written it, but what matters is that it be clear and engaging to the reader. The editor's job is to help the writer see what is working in a manuscript and what is not.

Kara wrote Kate some notes about suggested changes, and Kate made the revisions. Kara loved the new version of *Winn-Dixie* even more than the first. "I wrote another impassioned plea because I still didn't have the power to call Kate myself and make her an offer," Kara remembered. This time, Kara's boss said, 'Yes. Let's buy this book,' and she put Kara in charge of getting *Winn-Dixie* into print.

"It was incredible generosity on Liz's part that she allowed me to edit the book, because I had never edited anything before," Kara said. "But she saw how passionate I was and knew how much I had invested."

So the first-time editor and the first-time novelist worked together to polish Kate's manuscript over the coming months. The version of *Because of Winn-Dixie* that was published in March 2000 was Kate's eighth (and final) draft.

Kate knew from working at the Bookman that most middle-grade novels sell very modestly, so she had humble expectations for what would happen once she became a published author. Publishers typically give an author an advance when they acquire a novel. For a first-time children's novelist, the advance would typically be $10,000 or less. The author earns royalties on the sale of each book, but the publisher does not pay the author any additional money until it has earned back the amount of the advance.

"I had one fervent hope," Kate said, "and that was that the book would sell five thousand copies, so I would earn back my advance and be allowed to write another book. That was really all I wanted."

Kate DiCamillo

The Tiger Rising

FROM THE AUTHOR OF
THE NEWBERY HONOR BOOK
BECAUSE OF WINN-DIXIE

Kate's second novel
was a finalist for the
National Book Award.

Chapter 3
THE TIGER RISES

The first indication that *Because of Winn-Dixie* would not only earn back its advance but also become a hit was a review that appeared in *Publishers Weekly*, a magazine that booksellers read to help them decide which books to stock in their stores. The review called Kate's book "an exquisitely crafted first novel."

"Getting a starred review is always good, but this was more than that. It was a starred review that was an absolute rave," Kara remembered. Two other important magazines—*School Library Journal* and *Kirkus Reviews*—also gave *Winn-Dixie* starred reviews.

Kara was only too happy to buy another manuscript from Kate. Editor and author worked together to revise Kate's second book, *The Tiger Rising*, which was also set in rural Florida.

The main character of *The Tiger Rising* is Rob Horton, whose mother recently died. Like Opal, he is new in town. He does not find a dog at a grocery store. Instead he finds a tiger, in a cage, in the woods behind the motel where he and his father live. Rob shares this secret knowledge with the first friend he makes, a girl named Sistine who rides his bus. Their agreement that the tiger should be freed solidifies their friendship.

The Tiger Rising and *Because of Winn-Dixie* share themes. In her first two books, Kate explores the impact of a loss or absence of a parent on kids, the importance of friendship, and the crucial role animals can play in children's lives.

Thanks to the success of *Winn-Dixie*—and to a $25,000 grant she won from a local arts council to support her writing—Kate was able to switch from her full-time job at the book warehouse to a part-time job at a used bookstore. This gave her more time to write without having to sacrifice one of her favorite perks at the Bookman: reading on the job.

Things were really looking up for Kate, who had been so disappointed in herself in the decade after her college graduation. She was thirty-six and seemed to have it all—one book published, another on the way, a wide circle of good friends in the place she now called home, an adequate number of warm socks, and a winter coat—when the phone rang in her Minneapolis apartment on the morning of January 15, 2001.

On the other end was Caroline Parr, the chair of the Newbery Committee. The committee had chosen *Because of Winn-Dixie* for a Newbery Honor—a runner-up to the highest prize in children's literature. Just like Christopher Paul Curtis, whose first novel, *The Watsons Go to Birmingham—1963*, had inspired Kate to write for kids in the first place, Kate had won a Newbery Honor for her first novel.

Kate never had to worry about earning back her advance. *Winn-Dixie* would go on to sell 7.5 million copies over the next decade. Kate's first novel would be translated into twenty-eight languages.

Kate, who says her natural state is "worried," was relieved that she'd already turned in the manuscript for her second book, *The Tiger Rising,* by the time the call came from the Newbery Committee. After the call, she was very much in demand. But, as it turned out, *The Tiger*

Rising was destined to be singled out for excellence, too. In October 2001, it was named a finalist for the National Book Award, another prestigious prize.

"I felt like the luckiest person in the world," Kate said.

Promoting her books has sent Kate all over the world, including to England, where she visited the Tower of London.

Chapter 4
A FAIRY TALE COMES TRUE

Most writers would be thrilled if their first novel won a Newbery Honor and their second was a finalist for the National Book Award, and Kate definitely was happy.

She was also terrified.

"I spent a long time trying to write another book like *Winn-Dixie*," she remembered. "That did not work."

Could Kate produce another book readers would love?

She needed an idea. She got one from a very unlikely source.

Luke Bailey was eight years old in 2001. He was the son of Kate's best childhood friend, Tracey Bailey. He had an idea for Kate. He wanted her to write a story about "an unlikely hero with exceptionally large ears."

Kate laughed but quickly set him straight. "You're asking the wrong person. That's not the way I write stories."

And yet, Kate found she could not get the phrase "unlikely hero" out of her head. Thus was born Despereaux Tilling, a tiny mouse with oversize ears, a rodent so pitifully small that his mother, Antoinette, names him for a word that sounds to her like "disappointment." (In addition to being a terrible mother, Antoinette is very bad at French. The French word for "disappointment" is *désappointement*.)

Despereaux would have to rescue someone in order to be an unlikely hero, so Kate cooked up a maiden in distress: Princess Pea, whose mother dies of fright at the sight of a rat in her soup. There would also have to be villains: the rat, Roscuro, and his unwitting accomplice, a peasant girl named Miggery Sow.

It was an ambitious story, told in parts from separate points of view—and definitely not anything like the two books Kate had already written and published with Candlewick Press.

"She sent me about thirty pages, and I told her 'Keep going,'" editor Kara LaReau remembered. "I wasn't fazed by the difference between Despereaux and the other books, but Kate was. What I saw was another story with amazing potential that already reflected her high level of craftsmanship."

Then world events almost stopped Kate from continuing. She was visiting her mother in Florida on September 11, 2001, the day terrorists hijacked four planes and used them to attack New York City and Washington, D.C. Thousands of innocent people were killed. It was one of the grimmest days in American history.

Later that week, when Kate was on her way home to Minneapolis, a man sitting next to her asked her what she did for a living. She said she was a writer.

"What are you working on now?" he asked. Kate sheepishly admitted she was writing a fairy tale.

"I was mortified," Kate recalled. "Here the world was falling down around us, and I'm trying to tell the story about a mouse who saves a princess. I said, 'It doesn't matter at all now.'"

But while Kate was waiting for her luggage at the baggage carousel, the man approached her. "Maybe you're wrong," he said. "Maybe stories do matter."

Kate wrote the man's words on a scrap of paper and taped it above her desk. When she struggled with the manuscript, she would glance at the quotation to remind herself that, even at our darkest hour, stories matter.

She looked at those words *a lot.* "I had sent this two-ounce mouse down into a dungeon with a sewing needle to save a human princess and had no idea how in the world he was going to do it. I thought I would never make my way through it. I had no outline. It kept getting increasingly complicated. If you look at the rough drafts, there's a lot of blood on those pages."

Somehow, she got to "The End." The book was released in August 2003. It received even more starred reviews than *Winn-Dixie* had.

On January 12, 2004, the phone rang again, this time in Kate's house. Her success had allowed her to move from an apartment to a house—a place big enough for Kate to have a dog!

This time it was a lady named Eliza Dresang calling, and her news was slightly different from the news Kate had gotten the last time. Kate had not won a Newbery Honor.

The Tale of Despereaux had won the Newbery Medal.

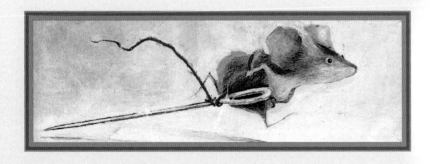

Kate created the mouse Despereaux Tilling after her son's friend asked for a story about "an unlikely hero with exceptionally large ears."

Ten Questions about *The Tale of Despereaux*

Q: Your mother's not anything like Despereaux's, is she? She wouldn't adjust her makeup as you were being led to your death, would she?

Kate: I love my mother. Write that down.

Q: But a reader might wonder if you have something against mothers—Opal's is gone, Rob's and Princess Pea's are dead, and Despereaux's mother should have been stopped from having mice.

A: I get this question a lot, and this time I said, "I can't let that happen again. I must take care of the mothers." But the story will do what the story wants. It was out of my control.

Q: The reader might also wonder if there's more than a little of the author in Despereaux, the tiny, sickly mouse who loves to read. That sounds like your childhood.

A: There's more of me in this book—more that I'm aware of—than any other book, but that's because I'm the narrator. That's me. And I certainly empathized with Despereaux when he was going down into the dungeon because that's how I felt every morning when I started writing. I never know what's going to happen in my stories and, with this one, I had all these pieces and no idea how I was going to make it all work.

Q: Your curly hair isn't hiding incredibly large ears like Despereaux's, though, is it?

A: Write down that I have normal ears.

Q: Despite the fairy-tale setting, Despereaux seems to have had the modern misfortune of being born to a dysfunctional family.

A: That's an interesting point. I intentionally included details that make the story of this time. The king plays a guitar, not a lute. And Miggery Sow's father sells her for cigarettes, which are modern things. But yes, you could say Despereaux's family is dysfunctional, although I didn't set out to write a story about dysfunctional families.

Q: The guitar and the cigarettes notwithstanding, the story has a nineteenth-century air with all the asides from the narrator. Have you been reading Lemony Snicket?

A: Mostly what I read was Dickens, who doesn't address the reader directly, but that's who I was tipping my hat to. I had this quote of his taped above my computer: "Make them laugh, make them cry, but most of all, make them wait."

Q: I also see the influences of Scheherazade. What kinds of stories does Despereaux tell Gregory [the jailor in the dungeon] to stay alive?

A: Hmm. I don't know what stories he told him. But that would be a good exercise if you were using the book in the classroom. I guess what I think is that Despereaux's whole story is a testament to the power of story.

Q: This book is quite the departure for you. It's not written in the Southern voice your readers have come to know and love.

A: People have told me it's darker than I realized. I thought it was a funny book. I know that talking to the reader directly is out of fashion. I worried about that. And there are about a million mouse stories. But I had to write this story. I wasn't going to be able to write anything else until I wrote this.

Q: In *Despereaux*, the narrator says, "Love is ridiculous." Do you really believe love is ridiculous?

A: And powerful and wonderful. Same with hope and forgiveness. You look at the world and you think it's ridiculous to hope, but it's also powerful and wonderful to hope.

Q: How about Happily Ever After? Is there such a thing?

A: There is such a thing, but it's never the happily ever after we initially envision. Sometimes it's better.

Kate appears at the Los Angeles premiere of the film based on her book, *A Tale of Despereaux.*

Chapter 5
HOLLYWOOD!

Winning three big awards for your first three books brings a writer a lot of publicity. Some of the people who now began paying attention to Kate's work were film producers. Kate's publisher sold the rights to make a movie based on *Because of Winn-Dixie*, as well as *The Tale of Despereaux*. The film rights to Kate's fourth novel, *The Miraculous Journey of Edward Tulane*, were sold before the book was even published!

For Kate, the experience was almost unreal. The director of *Winn-Dixie*, Wayne Wang, asked her to come to San Francisco, where he lived, so he could pick her brain about the characters she had created. "Before I knew it, I was writing a screenplay," she said. "It was a very good experience because I'm always fearful of trying new things. I had to tell myself to fight that fear and go out there and see if you can just learn."

Kate also got to visit the set in Napoleonville, Louisiana, a rural town that closely resembles the fictional town of Naomi, Florida. She arrived while they were filming the scene in the pet shop where Otis, played by the popular singer Dave Matthews, lets all the animals out of their cages for a concert.

"If you'd have told me when I was up at 4:30 in the morning making up that scene that five years later I'd be watching Dave Matthews bring it to life, I would have said you were crazy," Kate said.

Released in 2005, the film stars Jeff Daniels, Cicely Tyson, Eva Marie Saint, and AnnaSophia Robb as Opal. A Picardy shepherd was imported from France to play Winn-Dixie. The dog had no prior acting experience but had the right look: lovable rascal.

In 2008, *The Tale of Despereaux* hit theaters as a computer-animated film. Big stars like Matthew Broderick, Dustin Hoffman, and Emma Watson voiced the main characters.

Four, almost identical, Picardy Shepherds were imported from France to play the title role in the movie version of Kate's book, *Because of Winn-Dixie.*

But even more important than having films made from her books, the success of Kate's first three novels allowed her the freedom to try her hand at whatever kind of writing she might like. Her friend Alison McGhee's love of buttered toast gave her an idea for a chapter-book series about the porcine wonder Mercy Watson. She wrote one picture book about Christmas—*Great Joy*—and another about a chicken. And she wrote a fourth novel, inspired by a china rabbit given to her by Jane Resh Thomas, whose writers' group had encouraged Kate to keep at it when she was new to Minneapolis. *The Miraculous Journey of Edward Tulane,* released in 2006, won the Boston Globe-Horn Book Award for fiction, another prestigious prize.

Perhaps what best illustrates how far Kate had come was how different the release of *Edward Tulane* was from the publication of her first book. When *Because of Winn-Dixie* was published in 2000, there was no author tour and little fanfare. The release party for *Edward Tulane* was too big for any bookstore to host. Instead it was held at the Fitzgerald Theater in St. Paul—and even that wasn't big enough! A standing-room-only crowd of fans lined up down the block and around the corner two hours before showtime—in February, in Minnesota—because seating was first-come, first-served.

"When I came out on stage, there was a whole lot of applause and I thought I was going to cry," Kate remembered. "But, after that, the whole evening is sort of a blur. It was just astonishing."

Kate writes her novels and stories in a book-filled office in her Minneapolis home.

Chapter 6
WHAT'S NEXT FOR KATE?

Astonishing is the perfect word to describe what has happened to Kate since the publication of her first book in 2000. She would be the first person to tell you that.

Kate cannot share the secret of her success. She claims to have no idea.

"I'm not being disingenuous when I say I don't know what I'm doing," she insists. "I'm just biting my nails and hoping to be true to the voice I hear in the story."

When pressed, Kate offers this advice to aspiring writers: "Listen, write, read. And eavesdrop. I do a lot of eavesdropping." Kate has trained herself to write down ideas or images that come to her no matter where inspiration strikes. In a dream about the china rabbit her friend Jane gave her, she saw him on the ocean floor. From that image alone, Kate spun out a whole book!

In 2009, Kate published a fifth novel, *The Magician's Elephant*. (She got the idea for this book while standing in the lobby of a hotel in New York City.) In 2010, she branched out again and coauthored *Bink & Gollie*, an easy-reader book, with her friend Alison McGhee.

"I entered into the whole [coauthor] enterprise reluctantly because that's not the way I work," Kate said. "But working with another writer—

that opens up other doors in your brain." Her risk was rewarded when *Bink & Gollie* won the Theodor Seuss Geisel Award (named for Dr. Seuss), a prize given to the year's best book for beginning readers. The second book in the Bink & Gollie series, *Bink & Gollie: Two for One*, was published in 2012.

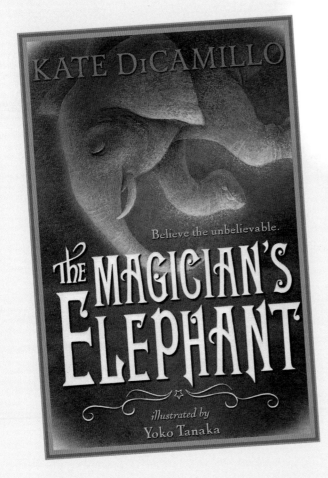

In *The Magician's Elephant*, an impossible prediction by a fortune-teller comes true.

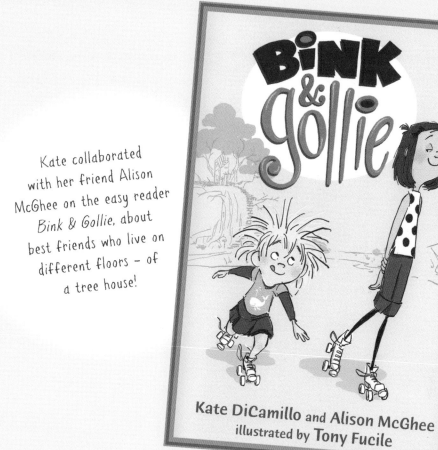

Kate collaborated with her friend Alison McGhee on the easy reader *Bink & Gollie*, about best friends who live on different floors – of a tree house!

Kate DiCamillo and **Alison McGhee**
illustrated by **Tony Fucile**

Some successful writers would play it safe. For Kate, on the other hand, success has provided the confidence to take a few more chances than her nature would normally dictate.

What hasn't changed is Kate's need to write. Two pages a day. Monday through Friday. When she's home in Minneapolis, she enjoys the company of Henry, her part-time dog, who lives with another family when Kate is traveling.

Life simply makes more sense to Kate when she writes about it. Not writing is not an option. "[Writing] does clarify things. I don't need to do it for the money anymore," she said. "The urge to write, to tell a story—that desire is independent from the need to make a living. The desire to find a story to tell stands alone."

KATE LIKES TO READ:

Kate spent many hours of her childhood at the Cooper Memorial Library in downtown Clermont, where Miss Alice, the children's librarian, fed her a steady diet of rich reading. Kate advises anyone who wants to be a writer to consume as many books as possible. You'll find some of these books, her favorites, in your school or public library.

The Mouse and the Motorcycle by Beverly Cleary

Ribsy by Beverly Cleary

The Twenty-One Balloons by William Pène du Bois

The Borrowers series by Mary Norton

The Cricket in Times Square by George Selden

Little House on the Prairie (and everything else) by Laura Ingalls Wilder

BOOKS BY KATE DICAMILLO

Chapter Books

The *Bink & Gollie* books (with Alison McGhee), illustrated by Tony Fucile
(Candlewick Press, 2010 and 2012)

The *Mercy Watson* books, illustrated by Chris Van Dusen (Candlewick
Press, 2005)

Novels

Because of Winn-Dixie (Candlewick Press, 2000)

The Tiger Rising (Candlewick Press, 2001)

The Tale of Despereaux (Candlewick Press, 2003)

The Miraculous Journey of Edward Tulane (Candlewick Press, 2006)

The Magician's Elephant (Candlewick Press, 2009)

Picture Books

Great Joy, illustrated by Bagram Ibatoulline (Candlewick Press, 2007)

Louise, the Adventures of a Chicken, illustrated by Harry Bliss (Harper, 2008)

GLOSSARY

advance—Money provided to an artist or creator (such as a writer, illustrator, or performer) before the work of art makes a profit.

cadence—The rhythmic flow of sounds or language.

carte blanche—Unrestricted power to act at one's own discretion.

discretion—The quality of being selective. (When Kate says she read "without discretion," she means she read everything she found in front of her no matter what it was.)

dysfunctional—Impaired or abnormal.

maternity leave—An absence from work given to mothers in order to care for newborn babies. Some employers also provide paternity leave for fathers.

reader reports—Written assessments outlining the strengths and weaknesses of a particular manuscript.

royalties—Money that an author or illustrator receives from the sale of each copy of a book. Most authors receive 10 percent of the retail price for each book sold ($1.60 for every $16 book).

salutatorian—The student with the second highest grade point average in a graduating class. The student with the highest grade point average is the valedictorian.

Scheherazade—The fictional wife of the sultan in *The Thousand and One Nights*. She avoids the fate of the sultan's previous wives by telling him part of a mesmerizing story every night and promising to finish it the next night.

starred review—A critique indicating a book of outstanding quality.

CHRONOLOGY

March 25, 1964: Katrina Elizabeth DiCamillo is born at Lankenau Hospital in Wynnewood, PA.

1969: Kate, her brother, and her mother move to Clermont, FL.

1982: Kate delivers the salutatorian address as she graduates from Clermont High School.

1987: Kate graduates from the University of Florida in Gainesville with a degree in English.

1994: Kate moves to Minneapolis and takes a job in a book warehouse.

1998: Kate wins a grant from the McKnight Foundation to support her writing, which allows her to quit her full-time job at the warehouse. She gets a part-time job at a used bookstore.

March 2000: *Because of Winn-Dixie* is published by Candlewick Press.

January 15, 2001: The American Library Association names *Because of Winn-Dixie* a Newbery Honor Book.

October 2001: *The Tiger Rising* is named a finalist for the National Book Award.

January 2004: *The Tale of Despereaux* wins the 2004 John Newbery Medal.

August 2005: Kate's first chapter book, *Mercy Watson to the Rescue*, is published.

June 2006: *The Miraculous Journey of Edward Tulane* wins the Boston Globe-Horn Book Award for fiction.

December 2008: An animated film version of *The Tale of Despereaux* opens in theaters.

September 2009: Kate's fifth novel, *The Magician's Elephant,* is published.

January 2011: *Bink & Gollie*, written with Alison McGhee and illustrated by Tony Fucile, wins the Theodor Seuss Geisel Award.

FURTHER INFORMATION

Books

Are you interested in trying to write stories yourself? These two books offer guidance:

Levine, Gail Carson. *Writing Magic*. New York: Collins, 2006.

Messner, Kate. *Real Revision: Authors' Strategies to Share with Student Writers*. Portland, ME: Stenhouse, 2011.

Websites

www.katedicamillo.com

www.candlewick.com/katedicamillo

www.binkandgollie.com

www.themagicianselephant.com

www.mercywatson.com

BIBLIOGRAPHY

A note to report writers from Sue Corbett

To write this biography, I read all of Kate's books and did research online by reading articles that other journalists have written about her. I had interviewed Kate myself several times in my role as the children's book reviewer for the *Miami Herald*, but after I compiled a list of questions that my research hadn't answered, I interviewed her again. I also spoke to Kate's editor, friends, booksellers, and librarians.

Below is a list of sources that I used. Anytime *you* write a report, you should also keep track of where you got your information. It is fine to use information in your report if you found it somewhere else, as long as you give the source credit in a footnote, endnote, or note within the report itself. (Your teacher can tell you how he or she prefers you to list your sources.)

It is not okay to pass off other people's work as your own. Just ask Kate to tell you about the time she copied a story out of *Humpty Dumpty Magazine*. . . .

PRINT ARTICLES

"Author's Got Her Own Cinderella Tale," by Sue Corbett, *Miami Herald*, March 11, 2006, p. 1E.

"Brand New Tail: A Big-Eared Mouse Follows Big Cat," by Sue Corbett, *Miami Herald*, Sept. 6, 2003, p. 1E.

"Pleasantly Stunned, A Star Children's Author Hits the Tour Trail Again," by Jane Margolies, *The New York Times*, Feb. 21, 2006, p. D1

"Sometimes Fairy Tales Really Can Come True," by Sue Corbett, *Miami Herald*, Jan. 15, 2005, p. 1E.

"Third Time's the Charm," by Jan Annino Godown, *Florida*, Winter 2005, pp. 22–23.

"When Elephants Dance," by Adam Gopnik, *The New York Times Book Review*, Dec. 6, 2009, p. 46.

"A World without Soup," by Jerry Griswold, *The New York Times Book Review*, Nov. 16, 2003, p. 47.

ONLINE VIDEO

Kate DiCamillo: MNOriginal, produced by Twin Cities Public Television, 2010. Accessible online at www.mnoriginal.org/art/?p=2280.

Kate DiCamillo interview by Stacey Cochran for Raleigh Television Network program *The Artist's Craft*. Accessible online at http://wn.com/Kate_DiCamillo.

ONLINE AUDIO

Kate DiCamillo reads from *The Miraculous Journey of Edward Tulane*, Feb. 14, Fitzgerald Theater, Minneapolis, MN. Available at Minnesota Public Radio's website: http://minnesota.publicradio.org/display/web/2006/02/14/dicamillo/

INDEX

ABOUT THE AUTHOR:

Sue Corbett is a reporter who has worked for the *Miami Herald*, *People* magazine, and *Publishers Weekly*. She is also the author of several novels for kids, including *The Last Newspaper Boy in America*, *Free Baseball*, and *12 Again*.